All Scripture references taken from the KJV of the Holy Bible, unless otherwise indicated.

Second Marriage, Third Marriage, *any* Marriage

by Dr. Marlene Miles

Freshwater Press, 2023

ISBN: 978-1-960150-80-6

Paperback Version

Copyright 2023 by Dr. Marlene Miles

All rights reserved. No part of this book may be reproduced, distributed or transmitted by any means or in any means including photocopying, recording or other electronic or mechanical methods without prior written permission of the publisher except in the case of brief publications or critical reviews.

Contents

Introduction 5
This Is Too Expensive 9
Enchante' 13
Get Divorced First 16
Fix You 20
Prayer for Healing After Divorce 21
Kingdom Marriage 23
Prayer for the Wrong Guy 25
Where Is His Ex? 26
He's Got Sole Custody 30
The Widower 39
Polygamous Mate 41
Polygamous Killers 47
With Your Life 57
Spirit Spouse 62
Divorcing Spirit Spouse 71
Spirit Children 74
So Much *Marine* Out There 75
Secrets 79
Previous Children 80

Second Marriage
Third Marriage
any
Marriage

Freshwater Press, USA

Inheritance	81
Marriage *Material*	83
With Permission	86
Pro-Marriage	90
Prayers	92
Prayers Against Late Marriage/ Marital Delay	93
Christian books by this author	97

Introduction

More than 40 million people in the US have been married more than once. 125 million are married now and about 5% of those are married for their third time, or more. If you are going into a second or third, marriage or more... what do you need to look out for spiritually?

To your shock, disappointment, and bittersweet joy, it's your second marriage. God would not do away with the first, except to establish the second, or something better in your life. **What do you need to know now**? What do you need to look for when remarrying, for a second or third marriage, or *more*? If God is in it, let go of feelings of guilt, and fear. Are you the one looking at another marriage? Or has *he* had multiple marriages? Maybe both of you have.

This book, **Second Marriage, Third Marriage,** *any* **Marriage** is written to women who may be embarking on another marriage but there is no reason why men can't make use of it; just change the gender as you read. It will focus on the second or third marriage but can be handy in vetting your intended for *any* marriage. If you are normal, you are planning that your first marriage will be your *only* marriage, but with the divorce rate over 50%, even in the church, seems life doesn't always work out that way.

It is in no way written to cast aspersions on the good guys, but things seem to get a little more complicated, as time goes by, and we move from relationship to relationship. Ladies, if you don't get married in the first round--, around high school or college age, you may find that later on, the choices are completely different. You may not feel that you even have choices; where do you even meet others? In your 20's seems everywhere you go there is somebody who is interested in you or wanting to date you. Later, when we are not in school and on campuses with large quantities of people, where are the eligible ones, now? With Covid and people shut in all over the place, some haven't even come back out to socialize as they used to; many have. So, meeting new, available people may be complicated now. Those who may be available physically, that is single-unmarried, or single-divorced may be unavailable or even unacceptable in other ways. *Keep reading*

For this reason, I recommend that women and men seek to be married in their twenties, work on your marriage, **stay** married, and build for your future, to the Glory of God.

In the second and third rounds of getting matched up and married, women (and men) need to keep their eyes open and pay attention to details. Every detail.

Anyone can experience the frustration of trying to find the right one, the right conditions, the right situation. Yet, we all aspire to that Kingdom Marriage, that one and only.

This book could be useful to answer a lot of questions or confirm things you may already know or suspect. Or, you could get a jump on the devil and read it before you ever marry anyone and get yourself really prepared to be married for a long healthy life together.

Both of you want the kingdom marriage, *right*? This book can be a part of your preparation.

This Is Too Expensive

Divorce is entirely too expensive. Getting married is expensive, but divorce costs even more. Not just in money, but in momentum, time, emotional upheaval, as well as financial losses.

Our God is a God of multiplication. He says, ***Be fruitful and multiply***. Multiplication brings abundance and prosperity. We are supposed to be multiplying in the Earth. Divorce is division; it is the opposite of multiplication, and it is not of God.

God hates divorce, the breaking of covenant, but He allows it. Back in Moses' time, the men were either putting their wives away, because they wanted a new one; or, like ID Discovery, men were killing their wives.

Centuries later, seems humans are still the same. There are men who want **no** children and there are too many reports of things happening to both pregnant wives and pregnant women--, mistresses and girlfriends. The motives for such vary as much as the devil can think up and put into the mind of a susceptible perpetrator.

Henry VIII is famous for having killed two of his six wives. When a woman is only as important as what she looks like, or if she can't magically reject the man's X chromosome to *only* take the Y-chromosome of the man's XY combination to make a male child, then an ignorant man will think she is worthless. Y Chromosomes make males; the woman has **no** Y chromosome; she has two X chromosomes, that's what makes her a woman. The man has an X and a Y; each supply one chromosome to the baby. Therefore, **he** must supply the Y to make a male child.

Without designer babies and genetic manipulation, better pray to God to get the gender you want; your wife is not God.

Putting away was declaring your wife unfit, or unacceptable and a woman could end up being stoned, out in the street, exiled out of the community with nowhere to go or live, even with children, if the man, on a whim, decided he wanted to be rid of her. Putting away is not the same as giving a bill of divorcement, and if not officially and legally divorced, technically both the man and the woman are *still married,* so in their next relationships, they are committing adultery.

This is what a divorced person who marries is committing adultery verse really means in the Bible. (Luke 16:18)

God **does** allow divorce.

In the OT, a woman could leave a husband if he didn't give her *due benevolence,* a place to live and tend to her financial needs. Not the other way around, as a lot of men seem to think these days. Today's reversal of gender responsibilities is rather troubling to me. It could be related to males seeing their "single mothers" do everything in a household, so they have no idea what a man is supposed to do, so they think he does nothing.

Men, who have abandoned wives and children, read that again.

Women are guilty of spoiling their male children, as men are guilty of overindulging their daughters. Facts.

Divorce is expensive because it is **division**; it is the opposite of multiplication. If being fruitful goes with multiplication, then the opposite happens with division. Each parent is not running another household. There are children and they are expensive. Divorce lawyers are not cheap, either.

Fast forward to retirement age, divorced people have probably had more upheaval, struggles, and money issues than the man who drew waters from his own cistern all his life and stayed with the faithful wife of his youth to build a home, a family, a retirement plan, equity, and a legacy. It's not that some people have all the luck; some people do all the **work**. They stayed married and build a life for themselves and children, without killing each other.

People who stay married live longer than lone wolves, men out on the prowl. Notwithstanding Covid, we hear that hospitals have their share of sick men, who aren't that old, but have no one. No one. They fell for the devil's lies that they didn't need anyone, not a wife, not a family. So now that he's sick and/or old, he is alone and has no one.

Enchante'

But whether you were looking or not, you met someone new. Whether you were set up on a blind date, or happenstance--, it doesn't matter how you met; you met.

So nice to meet you, he may say.

Why is *this guy* single, you may ask yourself. He is a zaddy; how exciting! Cool your jets, settle down and put on your discernment. Discern every *spirit*. **Is he human? No? *Run*.**

Does he have a heart? Is he capable of love? Don't waste your time if he is incapable of love or emotionally unavailable. No matter what he has or appears to have, if he has no love, he has **nothing**, (1 Corinthians 13); he *is* nothing, a vapor.

Is he a narcissist? ***Run***. On your own, you will never rehabilitate a narcissist because as far as they see, there is nothing wrong with them, so, there's nothing to fix. If they won't let Jesus fix it, what do you think you're going to do? *Love* him out of it? He doesn't know what love is, therefore, he cannot give it or receive it. A man without Jesus automatically has no love. Sure, you can minister to him if the Lord says so. Marry him? Ask the Lord, and listen.

What is his spiritual status? Does he *have* a spiritual status? What **God** is he serving? Does he acknowledge one God, Jehovah, or does he spout off a lot of different words calling the names of popular religions and false *gods* to make you believe that he believes in **all** of them or *most* of them, or can be encouraged to believe in whatever you believe in just to earn your trust?

If he says he confesses Christ, what is his relationship with God right now? Is he okay? Or are things going so badly in his life that you take pity and want to help him? Did God say help him? Did you ask God if this man is under spiritual judgment from God right now? If he is, do you want to tie your star to that? Unless God anoints and sends you, you won't pull him up; he will drag you down. How do you expect to fight or overcome God's judgment on a man?

He's good looking, but get real.

You may be well positioned in your life, well established in your career and comfortable. You may have hobbies and friends and are really not looking for anyone. And, that's when they show up, when you're not looking.

Or, you could be so tired of being alone. In that case you don't have peace. When you are not in a position of peace, at any time of your life, that is **not** the time to be looking for or entering into a serious, long-term, emotional, romantic relationship. If you don't have peace, or are feeling desperate, that's a dangerous time; that's when the devil can really trick and ensnare a person.

Get Divorced First

As costly as it is, if you are divorced or had to become divorced, so be it.

But, before you can enter into another relationship, you've got to get fully divorced from the previous spouse. Yes, legally divorced, but you've got to get divorced *spiritually* and break all soul ties. When you break up with a guy, it takes more than to just stop seeing or having sex with him to break up with him. You've got to also break the soul tie.

The same goes for divorcing someone that you were legally married to. Of course, what God has joined together, let no man tear it asunder. A three-fold cord is not easily broken (Ecclesiastes). With either a marriage, or a soul tie, it's going to be much harder to break it than it was to form it.

Until you are divorced from a person, or an *idol*, for that matter, you are still connected and responsible for performing whatever you were performing, spiritually before you stopped seeing them. Unless a formal divorce has happened, or you will have to pay, *spiritually*.

Most difficulties in life are for not giving worship to the idol *gods* that you used to serve before you were saved. It's like not paying the fees on your time share. Getting away from these idols is like getting out of a timeshare – it's complicated, but it is doable. By all means, get saved, it is your only hope, but be ready to be a warrior for your full freedom and deliverance from all evil (Matthew 6:13).

Later in this book we will discuss *divorce* as it applies to divorcing idol *gods* and evil deities. That must happen too.

Prayer -Spiritual Divorce-Natural Spouse

Father, in the Name of Jesus I come to You to ask for a divorce from my spouse due to _____. We have navigated (or will navigate) the legal channels of this world for legal divorce of this land. But, Lord, what You join together, let no man tear apart. I believe you did join us together, so I must ask for a bill of divorcement against my spouse, whether I want to or not. Irreconcilable differences, emotional, physical abuse, lack of financial or emotional support, adultery--, whatever the reason. Father, You hate broken covenant and so do I but since the spouse no longer desires to dwell with me, I seek a divorce breaking all soul ties between us, in Jesus' Name.

I cancel every vow, promise and pledge made to him and ask you Lord to forgive me of unfulfilled vows, promises, and pledges and let there be no spiritual backlash or penalty because of this, in Jesus' Name.

Anything that threatens my covenant with You, Lord God, let that thing be dissolved, in the Name of Jesus.

Let every announcement and contract in the spirit that connects us as husband and wife, as one, be dissolved. We are no longer one, but we are individuals again, in Jesus' Name.

Lord, you said until death do us part; I proclaim death to this marriage, this relationship, in the Name of Jesus.

Make me single, make me a whole single again, in the Name of Jesus.

Remove all remorse, guilt, hatred and bitterness from me, in the Name of Jesus.

Lord, thank You for newness of life and may Your purposes in my life be fulfilled, let me reach destiny all to Your Glory, in the Name of Jesus, Amen.

Fix You

Now that you're divorced do your forensics on your relationship. If the entire break up was *his* fault, you are either a narcissist or bordering on narcissism and you won't change a thing about yourself.

You met him. Married him, stayed with him and maybe also had kids with him. What is it about you that attracts that kind of guy? Is it a foundational problem? I discuss this at length in my book, **Level the Playing Field.** Until you fix *you*, you will attract the same guy over and over. What is in your blood is what you will attract.

What made you stay with him?

You may not have liked things about your dad, but the men you meet are either like him or become like him over time. Fix you. Ask Jesus.

Prayer for Healing After Divorce

Lord, heal my heart, restore my soul, in the Name of Jesus.

Forgive me for any and every part I played in the breakup of this relationship/marriage and the breaking of covenant, which I believed You had joined together.

Lord, if I ignored the fact that You did not join our union together, please forgive me for ignorance or rebellion.

With You, all things are possible.

I bind the *spirits of unforgiveness*, *bitterness, guilt, sadness, sorrow*, and *resentment*, in the Name of Jesus. I bind the *spirit of jealousy* and/or anger over his new life, and/or new wife, in the Name of Jesus.

Lord, I choose to forgive, and I am sad for him that he has made this choice that I do not believe is right for his life, or mine, or ours or our children.

Lord, protect and guide our children to still be respectful, honor their parents and grow up in a balanced way, in the Name of Jesus.

Thank You for your lovingkindness and patience with me as I go through this process. Shorten the emotional pain and restore my joy, in Jesus' Name.

For this loss, this sorrow, this sadness, let me have joy in the morning. Let me keep my eyes on You and not on yesterday, in the Name of Jesus.

Kingdom Marriage

So, you're saved, and you've done the spiritual and emotional work to be a kingdom spouse, so now you want one. Well, Amen.

Maybe you've been saved all along, but married someone unsaved or unspiritual thinking you could change them. He said his name was Christian, so you thought that meant he was a Christian. Not always the case. Maybe you were married to a so-called Christian. Or, his name was Luke, and he was a lukewarm Christian. Was he saved, and a lazy Christian, a lukewarm Christian? Those are not candidates for Kingdom marriage.

A Kingdom marriage is put together by God and both parties submit to the Holy Spirit and the purposes of God for their lives.

Don't get tricked or stuck with a person who is disingenuous and is pretending to be a Christian because you are. Pretenders like that will go to church with you Sunday after Sunday until you marry them or football season starts, then they bow out because really, they want to watch the game. Which game? Any game. Every game. If you believe a non-Christian is a Christian, he's already playing the game, running it on you.

Married a fake-saved, backslidden, churched, but not saved or spiritual, or any combination of those descriptions? They may be churched and know the words to say. Here's a clue: Do they even *have* a Bible? What does it look like? Are the brand-new pages still sticking together? Does he have any other Bible-related books? Any material on Jesus or other spiritual matters, Christianity, or other "spiritual" things?

Look around his house. He's got a dream catcher, crystals, books on Feng Shui, religious masks from overseas that may or may not have been used in rituals, statues of idol *gods* because he thinks they look cool, and other witchy décor such as owls, fu dogs, salamanders, and runes lining his garden or front porch. He's wearing a freemason's ring, which he says was his dad's, and his arm is branded--, that's not a polio vaccine scar; he's a frat boy. You had better know the signs.

Nope, this is not it; he's not the one.

Prayer for the Wrong Guy

Lord, if he is among Your future saved, may he come into contact with those who will plant the seeds of the Kingdom and those who will water it, for only You can give the increase, in the Name of Jesus.

Lord for the sake of his life and for the sake of our children, I ask that someone come into his life and preach the Kingdom to him, in the Name of Jesus.

Thank You, Lord for letting me see that this is not the one and urging me by Your Spirit to move on, in the Name of Jesus.

Where Is His Ex?

Now you've met a new guy, things seem hopeful.

He's **had** a first wife? Where is she? Where is his ex? Even if she is bitter or hostile, it might be better to have to encounter her than for her to be absolutely no where around. Does she exist? Is she *alive*?

Second wife? Third? Is this a pattern? Does he suggest, or insist on you two getting life insurance, as soon as you are married, or even before? Oh, please, he won't say it like that. He will say, *__We__ should get insurance on ourselves for each other and our family, so if anything should happen, we will be taken care of.* And he will go buy insurance at the time you do, whether he keeps the policy in force, or not.

Serial groom? Black widower? And, in what way? Accidents? Mysterious deaths? It *just happened*, as in a demonic time bomb?

She got sick with 5 different illnesses that don't even run in her family. She's dead and everyone else in her family is alive and well. Sounds like the work of *spirit spouse*, or other idol *god*. Possibly an enchanter may have been hired or a witch he hooked up with took it upon herself to get rid of this man's wife so that man would be available to marry her. *(More on that later; w*e are still looking at him.)

Did he benefit from her death? How so? How did he benefit from *her* life? These things can be answered by the Holy Spirit, in prayer. You are praying, right? People are known all over the world to enter into devil agreements that don't just involve them. These agreements can involve other people they know, but these other people don't even know they are involved in any agreement. Close relations, wives, children, parents, without their knowledge can be targets. Spiritually, body parts, blood and bodily fluids of wives (and girlfriends) are employed in some kinds of money rituals, unbeknownst to the woman. Don't be that woman.

Oh, wow, he's rich; he's loaded. He's flush with cash; how did he get it? How does he get it? He gives you money but rather disrespects and disdains you? Doesn't want to touch you now that you're married? Yeah, we could call that *spirit spouse*, but any idol a person serves is a *spirit spouse*. Yup. If sex magic is part of his money ritual, he will not want to use up sexual "energy" on you. This is vile, but is this where the term, coming into money came from?

Cash cow? Why buy the cow if you can get money from it and it doesn't even know. A heartless man or the best actor in the world can fool another human if he's doing money rituals using her, to her demise. He doesn't even care what happens to her, as long as he gets money.

Seriously, you can tell if someone loves you or not, can't you? If not, you need Jesus, like yesterday. If someone does not LOVE you, honor and respect you, you'd be unwise to ***ever*** go to sleep in their presence. You've really got problems when you leave the doors of your house unlocked fearing less of intruders, than you do of the person you live with. So, you leave the doors unlocked, or are tempted to do so for a quick getaway should that be necessary.

Don't be that person.

But really, where is she, where is the ex-girlfriend, the ex-wife? Is she okay? Are the exes *okay*?

Idol *gods*, demons want blood, and eventually or ever so often, and regularly, they demand blood. Look at the lives of so many celebrities. Why don't they have happier lives? Where are their *relatives*???????

He's Got Sole Custody

So, we found out she *does* exist. She appears to be okay. We'll check on her again later, but let's check for the kids right now. The couple did divorce, but they have children. He has sole custody. How did he do *that*? Especially if the minor child is of tender years, younger than 4-years-old, favor is usually with the mother. Yes, women can be a hot mess, but you **must** look closely to be sure that she **is** a hot mess as to the reason he has full custody.

Men often say their exes are crazy. Did she start out "crazy" or did he make her that way? If she was crazy from the start, why did he marry her? Why was he with her? Why did he have kids with her? Either she wasn't crazy at first, or they both were.

You must find out how much he hates his ex-wife and the real reason why. If you are going to be his wife, the capacity to *hate a wife* has already been demonstrated by him. While you are observing how well he treats his mother and his sisters, as we've all been trained to observe, better see this: **If he can find ONE somebody to absolutely hate, and that person is not Satan, you need to reconsider who you are dealing with, knowing that he may be capable of turning on you**.

You should especially worry if he is trying to recruit *you* to hate his ex, along with him--, to gang up on her. Don't do that. His stories--, are they true? Are they? Is she that *bad*? He had no responsibility in their breakup? Learn to spot and admit when something is a lie. He married her. He stayed with her; he had kids with her. If she's really that bad, what must their children be like? Get ready to meet some bad kids, and they will be your step kids. This may be when the wars really begin. (Let us pray not.)

A narcissist will always run his ex down to his new "supply", (you), so if/when his ex begins to spill truth on him, her reputation is pre-tarnished, because he releases his version of the story **first**. Discern *spirits*; don't fall for this.

I've met too many men who don't want to pay child support with varying excuses. I've met men who don't want to pay child support because they feel it will end up in the hands of the ex-wife. They would be willing to hurt, even devastate their own children to hurt the ex-wife who is the **mother** of their children. One doesn't have to be an *ex*-wife to be mistreated. Again, he has established that he can be evil to a **wife**, and a **mother**--, of his own children, even. Knowing this, why would you want to be in either of those roles in his life?

I know men who need a wife (a new wife) to look **stable** in front of a judge so they can get custody of the child or children, so they will not have to give "that woman (the ex) a penny."

There are men who seek trophy wives. A trophy wife is chosen for her youth, beauty or both. She is an object. If he admires her then she's an idol. If he just brings her out from time to time, she's a toy. If, like Vashti she doesn't come out to strut and be displayed when he calls, she can be done away with and replaced.

Don't be that woman, either; trophies tarnish sooner than later.

And there are men who are looking for mothers for their children because the ex may have left him for any number of reasons. Is he looking for a *mother* for his children, or a wife, **or both**? Which one is he looking for the most? Are you applying to be the nanny? Or, do you think you are actually going to be a **wife** and get a **husband** in this connection?

I've met men who want to give the minor child the money and give the ex-wife nothing as if she's using the children as a money-making venture. Maybe in Hollywood, but in real life? Please. This guy who is only paying $200 a month for each child, as if the ex-wife is going on a shopping spree every month to buy $800 *red bottoms* and date every new man she sees.

There are real men who are looking for kingdom wives; I pray you meet that type instead of these others I am describing. If you've met a man who treats his ex with dignity and respect, you can't be jealous. Thank God and be a grown up yourself in this dynamic.

Men need to learn what is involved in taking care of a child; it is 24/7 and children eat a lot. Children outgrow clothes every month. Children want a lot of toys and games. Schools and school expenses are not cheap. Even if that man doesn't want to pay child support to the children's mother, the mother still needs to be taken care of somewhat in order to be <u>able</u> to take care of the child. Man: it's because of you that she has a child so you should pay toward that child's upbringing and upkeep.

If the mother is in dire straits, the child (children) will be also. If the child sees the mother struggling financially or in any other way suffering, then the child will be insecure, and also have no positive female role model at home. The dad's bad behavior gets in the bloodline and a daughter will bring home a man *just like dad*; it will be what she will attract, and it's all she will know.

The male child will become just like that man, or violently try to be the exact opposite of that man, unless something is done, by prayer, deliverance and right teaching.

If the child disrespects the mother, as the ex-husband may be demonstrating to their children by his egregious, angry behavior, and the child emulates their father, then the child enters into a **curse** for disrespecting his or her parent.

If the child eventually sees that the dad is being a jerk, absent the Grace of God, the child may disrespect **both** parents, for bringing them into *this*.

Now, this man has achieved what he thinks he wants: he's got partial or full custody of cute little kids. But these kids now have a curse on them, thanks to one or both parents. So, they are cute, little, cursed kids.

What does that mean? If you're **not** a cursed person but your kids are cursed, it can't transfer to you as in generational curses that transfer *forward*, but if you care anything about your kids, you will feel it. You will hurt when they hurt. Sickness and disease is part of the Curse of the Law. When your child is sick, you spend money to take them to the doctor or buy them meds. When your child is sick, you miss time from work. Your child may be sick at any time, or multiple times because they are under the Curse of the Law for disrespecting *one or both* parents, as they have been taught, sometimes inadvertently, but taught. You might be the parent that they disrespected, but **you** end up suffering along with them. This curse will follow your children all of their lives until they repent to God, break the curse and receive deliverance. When they have kids, the curse will transfer to your grandchildren.

If you have ever dishonored your own parents, now might be a good time for you to repent.

When your kids lack or are poor, you will either shell out money to them, or they will prop themselves up at your house and never leave, because they may not be able to afford to leave. Poverty is part of the Curse of the Law. If there are generational curses already running in your family, this will just load onto your kids and compound frustration and disaster in their lives.

Death is the third part of the Curse of the Law. It doesn't have to be physical death-, right away. But even looking at the news these days we see that too many young people seem not to be living out half their days, if we are promised 70 years and more, by reason of strength. It may not be physical death, it could be death of good things or opportunities in a child's life, for example. You can clearly see how having children is a *spiritual* thing, not just to have a cute kid to play with, dress up and post pictures online.

Even if these cute little cursed kids are your step kids, you will not only feel it, but you will also be affected by this as you watch your new husband's frustration and your household may lack while he gives, gives and gives to them. If you can see it and understand it, you will feel for him, and pray. If you are not spiritual and don't see it, you will become part of the problem as you moan and complain about how much he's spoiling his grown or minor kids, while not paying any attention to you or spending money on you! His kids are cursed, and he's trying to fix it with money. He's trying to fix a spiritual problem with a natural solution.

Eyes open, spiritual discernment, **ON** so you are not that person.

Nobody is perfect, but these are things to watch out for.

The Widower

He's a widower—this is tricky because if your heart strings are pulled, you'll be thinking how sad he must be. The children are motherless; that is unfortunate. Is he in deep grief? For how long? It's been 8 years. Can he get out of this grief? Does he have any spiritual wherewithal to be delivered from pining away and perpetual sorrow? If he's not letting Jesus do that for him, you may be marrying a very long-faced man who either can't get out of his sad cycle or plans to stay there.

Is this genuine, or is he milking this grief for attention, gifts, pies from the ladies at the church? Is he planning to be a perpetual widower? He may have found a way for that to work for him.

At my dental practice we encounter people who keep sorry teeth. They will do almost anything for you **not** to extract a broken down, hopeless tooth. Those bad teeth get them sympathy in terms of prescriptions from the next, new, unsuspecting dentist. Yeah, that's a thing. Drug seekers know it. Medical personnel know it too.

Sympathy? Attention seekers know how to use it.

Or, is he the perpetual widower as a way to stay non-committal?

He's a widower; what happened to *her*? How did she die? **Details. You'd better find out every detail.**

Polygamous Mate

If you are from a polygamous background but haven't done **a lot** of spiritual work and gotten deliverance, you will attract that, again and again. It's in the blood. You will attract the *spirits* that are like what's in your blood. Absent the Spirit of God, and walking by the Spirit, you will act out what comes naturally. What comes naturally is in your blood.

Does he have a bunch of old girlfriends, or ghosted lovers? Goes into equals married; anyone he's had sex with, even **once**, he's married to them and definitely there is a soul tie. If he's smooth and soave and has had a lot of experience – most likely he's been with a lot of women. Will he tell you his body count?

Some people who have never had sex with another can be soul tied. Soul ties can be formed emotionally as well. The longer a person lives, the more people they know the more likely they are to have one, two, or multiple soul ties. That's a two-way street, he may have multiple soul ties and the women he's dated may still be soul tied to him. If you both aren't going to break this in prayer, then get ready for anything.

Of course, he can't just dump all of his friends and start with a clean slate, but having agape friends will be the most supportive to your new relationship and marriage. Else, it's still polygamy and nobody likes polygamy except the one who has all the women chasing him.

Don't be deceived. Psychics, diviners, and second heaven powers and evil human agents who work for the kingdom of darkness, like to say if you're thinking of some guy, the guy you just met, the guy you are dating or just broke up with, it's because he's thinking of you. **That is not true. They are giving you false hope.** The devil can inspire thoughts in your head, 24/7, and the more you accept those thoughts, the more thoughts he will send you.

We all aspire to the kingdom marriage. When you meet your special person, it could be love at first sight. But there is also lust at first sight, so discern every *spirit*. But there is no such thing as the psychics' story of the *twin flames*.

In a pantheistic society, Plato, who also believed the Earth was flat, told this story, of Zeus, an idol Greek *god,* considered king of the *gods*. Hundreds of years before Christ, Plato said that humans once had four legs and arms and two faces. The *gods* felt threatened by this, so Zeus split the people in two; humans would wander in search of their other *half*—their *twin flame*. **Don't you believe that foolishness.**

Jehovah God does not split souls in two. He's got enough souls for each person who comes to Earth to have a whole soul. As a matter of fact, we are to protect and prosper our whole soul and present it to God in eternity. If God split souls, and He **doesn't**, but if He did, then in your quest to find your "twin flame" you'd really be finding yourself and marrying yourself. So don't be that person looking for something that is not even a thing.

A soul tie is an obsession, basically. Every evil soul tie includes the devil as the third cord of a threefold cord; bonds are strengthened by sexual covenants, and it is unholy. So if you or he were polygamous, you have married everyone you have ever slept with. You have to divorce them spiritually by breaking soul ties. Name them one by one.

Prayer to break soul ties: I release myself from all unprofitable relationships, in the Name of Jesus.

I bind all demonic authorities involved in my last relationship and I break the evil covenant that allows those demons into my life, by the power in the Blood of Jesus, in Jesus' Name.

I release myself from the hold of every bewitched relationship, in the Name of Jesus. I break every soul tie and demonic, inordinate, unrequited, useless affection toward my ex, or anyone else, in the Name of Jesus.

I break every desire and plot of the enemy to engage me in evil soul ties, and wasteful relationships that can go nowhere, in Jesus' Name.

I break every ungodly relationship, in the Name of Jesus. I renounce and break every soul tie I have had with my ex, every secret society, cults, frats, sororities, co-fornicators, adulterers, family members, and other organizations. Spouses, friends, former friends, acquaintances, fiances, doctors, clubs, and/or religious leaders, in Jesus' Name.

I renounce all hidden soul ties, including soul ties to things, stuff, places, times, events, music, food, et cetera, in the Name of Jesus.

I renounce, break and loose myself from all demonic subjection in my relationships, in the Name of Jesus.

I remove all mind controlling manipulations, daydreams and fantasies between me and my ex, and all other aforementioned people, in the Name of Jesus.

Let all evil affections be removed from my mind and blotted out by the Blood of Jesus, in the Name of Jesus.

Lord Jesus, I give you my emotions, my mind, take control of my affections and make them godly affections, in the Name of Jesus.

Lord, deliver my head, my mind, my entire soul so I can see clearly if I am in a soul tie that needs to be broken, in the Name of Jesus.

I unyoke myself from every satanic yoke and I distance myself in every way from every unrighteous relationship, in Jesus' Name.

Prayers to Break Evil Soul Ties

I claim complete deliverance from every soul tie in my life, in the Name of Jesus.

I release my ex to live his life and I release myself to live mine.

All cords between us are cut, all threefold cords between us are broken, unraveled, and severed, in the Name of Jesus. Amen.

Polygamous Killers

A man who has dated many women may have slept with at least one witch, and not even know it. They don't wear Goth clothes and pointed hats in the daytime or at nightclubs. She may be very beautiful and look like his dream girl. She might not even know she's a witch. Maybe she's not; it's her mother or her father who is casting the spells and making incantations. If he hurt that witch, or worse, jilted her and now notice that his life has not been going well ever since; that's a clue.

Or, you could have met a man who has cheated on his wife and gotten entangled with the witch of all witches. She decides she wants him, badly. Permanently.

Mysteriously this man's wife gets sick, sicker, and then sickest and dies. Really? I've seen it. That's why I asked the questions at the beginning of this book: Where is the former wife? What happened to her? If a man is under a witch's curse, that is a terrible thing. Sure, he doesn't believe in witchcraft, that's why he's the perfect candidate. **The witch must believe in witchcraft, not the victim.** The less that man believes in anything spiritual, especially God, the easier it is for that witch.

So, if he's ghosted a witch, that witch may have cursed his relationships, marriage, money, career--, anything really, and you decide to marry him. Oh boy! Unless you and he deal with this spiritually, together, get ready for trouble. This is especially difficult if he's not saved, is not spiritual, does not even think witchcraft exists, and won't even pray. Well, there you go.

This thing he doesn't believe in happened to his *wife, really to him and his whole family, but the wife is the one being taken out* because **he** was in the streets, sinning. The wife suffered; the wife got sick because the witch became obsessed with this man and wanted him to be single. Without the Holy Spirit telling you exactly what happened, what happened to his wife is a CLUE to the intent of the spell that was sent his way. That's why I asked at the beginning: **What happened to his wife?** Be forewarned.

You don't think witches do witchcraft for giggles, do you? This witch doesn't want to kill *him*, he's doing good to her flesh. She wants to kill the wife. But that's not always the case. This is so ID Discovery, you may say.

Oh, it's far worse than that.

As I began telling you earlier about the woman who had a philandering husband, but she is the one who got deathly ill. The wife began to suffer, but no one understood why. Putting his "good husband" hat back on, he and sick wife, though Baptist-saved, but living carelessly, they are both clueless, spiritually. They treat her sudden, non-generational sicknesses medically, *only*. The thought never occurred to them that these problems could be all spiritual.

Luke 13:16 says that Satan bound the woman for 18 years, so the devil can inspire or send sickness to people. The devil's human agents are witches, wizards and the like. For 18 years the doctors could not help the woman in the New Testament, she spent all she had and had become worse. Jesus was her only answer.

The woman with the adulterous husband who brought this "disease" home to her languished in and out of hospitals for about 10 years before she succumbed. They spent almost all they had saved in all their years of marriage. Married for 20 years, the first 10 years they were having children, the last 10, she was dying.

The witch? That adulterer and that witch still didn't marry. Why? He's too grief-stricken.

The altars that witches use, once activated are next to impossible to stop, without Jesus. So, even if the witch had a heart and then a change of heart, she can't just stuff those demons she summoned up from hell back into a jar and throw it in the ocean. The Bible tells us to destroy evil altars; if we are spiritual we know this and we do it.

First wife--, gone. Now, the next woman he gets with, **if he's serious about her**, she'll get hit with witchcraft attack, too. If she's unsaved and unspiritual, this evil is crouching at the door. The next woman, let's say she is saved and spiritual. Well, here comes a war.

And God will win.

I'm sharing all this to introduce you to what might be out there. Be wise, shrewd, discerning, with eyes and ears open and prayers hot to the Lord to know what you are dealing with. You may have met a charming *wild oats* sower who has been roaming and wandering about the planet for decades with no restraints. All that time he may be meeting, attracted to, dealing with and jilting people – men and women who also have ***no restraints***.

Prayer Points

In the Name of Jesus, I confess and repent of the sins of my parents and my ancestors. Lord, forgive me and them, in the Name of Jesus.

Lord, please remove all iniquity, break the curses of my bloodline, in the Name of Jesus.

All demons associated with, and in place to enforce the curse, be bound and paralyzed in the Name of Jesus.

Lord, reverse all damage done to spirit, soul, and body because of this curse, in Jesus' Name.

Because of this cheating man's polygamy, he has run up on a woman who is a witch; she is a killer. They come to steal, kill, and destroy. That's why they go to the devil, to get power to do evil. God doesn't license that kind of mayhem. Unopposed, witchcraft is very powerful.

Men, when you get into relationships you are primarily worried about your own hide, but what about your *wife; besides STD's what else are you bringing home to her*? What about your children and other relatives, like your parents; what might be the fallout that damages them, spiritually speaking? You didn't have *free* extra-marital sex and get away with it. That **never** happens.

He's a serial cheater, and that's bad enough; they say that never stops, so why would anyone want that kind of emotional heartache?

Man, if you're not married, what about your girlfriend? What about your previous girlfriends? If you get a hold of a jealous, insecure, power struck mistress who wants to exact vengeance or clear the way for what she wants, any of the people in your life, or formerly in your life are in peril. Period.

Men want to know what's wrong with women, why can't they get along? Several reasons.

1. Men. The woman's desire is to the man. (Genesis). She wants the man, and the other woman also wants the man, it's what makes Springer and Maury Povich shows. Women will fight over a man. Instead of the man making peace and being decent, he loves this. Men who like fights, don't care if women fight, and especially they don't care if women fight over them; it's humorous to a lot of men. But it is not harmless. Female feuds could go on and on and get very dangerous, even deadly, as discussed.

2. Men. Women are at war with one another sometimes, that's why they don't like each other. Sometimes these wars are caused by and promoted by males. Men, are naïve and want women to just get together and agree to get along. That's not how it works, men.

Women are spiritually sensitive, and they are picking up on vibes from the other woman that the man is not even noticing.

3. Polygamy. Polygamy is one of the chief things that leads to witchcraft. A jealous woman will make an enemy of another woman at a moment's notice. I write a great deal about this in my book about polygamy, **Too Many Wives:** *<u>Wonder Why You Have Lady Problems.</u>*

You'd better stay prayed up, so you don't become an unsuspecting enemy of a power struck, insecure, desperate, needy, man-hungry woman. Polygamy could bring out almost any kind of evil in a hurt, insecure, neglected, or fearful legal or sexual "wife."

I know another man who I believe is under a curse to not have **ANY** woman as a love interest. I wonder if it was because of a childhood vow he made--, but right now, every relationship goes to nothing. Dating or marriage--, it doesn't matter the type of love relationship, it ends. When this man embarks on romantic relationships--, his romantic interest has to get away from him or she will begin to feel that witchcraft. In one case, a woman actually died. I believe her death was collateral damage from unopposed witchcraft done against this unbelieving man. The woman who died was not a Protestant Christian believer who practiced her faith including spiritual warfare.

His inability to maintain a marriage or romantic relationships I do not believe is ancestral or generational because everyone else in his family is married and seemingly happy. Well, except him and his sister, who is the witch. She is soul tied to him; I don't know if it is mutual. She may be a *physical spirit spouse* to him without him being aware of it. There are non-sexual *spirit spouses*. Make of that what you will, for her to hate that her brother has a romantic relationship is twisted.

You just met a guy. Vett him; do your homework. Are his friends witches? Are his enemies witches? Don't borrow trouble, don't be collateral damage in an unsaved, unspiritual, clueless man's life. Are you prepared to come against a witch, or a coven of witches? Fear not, but are you called to fight the witches of *his* life? Then have at it. Else, you might reconsider this guy and guys like him who have **no spiritual acumen, prowess, or protection**. They seem big and bad, but these unprotected, prayerless men are like lambs for slaughter and if you are the spiritual one and he is not, then you will have to be his shepherd. Does any of that make sense to you, especially when the man is supposed to be the spiritual covering of a family?

With Your Life

They say that when it comes to dating, a first date especially, men are afraid of rejection and women are afraid of being murdered. Well, pay attention to this so you don't pay for a relationship with your life. I don't mean with an angry out of control gun-toting man, but maybe I do mean that. What I'm writing about in this chapter is more subtle, but can be deadly.

Don't be that person.

Money rituals are a thing. There are money rituals that a person could do on you, and you will never know they did anything to you. You especially won't notice if you are money struck, the guy has a lot of money, and he gives you large sums at a time. You will be too busy shopping to see the signs.

Sex magic is demonic, and it is real. In the book, **ESM, Evil Spirit Marriage** the author, Dr. Anthony Akerele mentions homosexual sex magic. Seems like that's a thing, too. So, no one is safe, except in living upright, and living a prayerful life, in Christ.

The things that people do and say and *yell* during sex, can be considered as initiations, *word curses, incantations and spells*. No kidding. More witchcraft, sex spells. Sex spells are real and are **NOT of GOD**. Illegal sex is bad enough, but if someone is telling you **what words** to use and what to say at certain times of the act—you should have already run out of there, but right now, RUN!

Every curse word invokes a demon, an idol *god*. Stop using that language--, those words. There is a story of a person who loved a certain *blank*-bomb word and used it regularly. The story is told that on a certain day this man was steeped in his favorite cuss words, a demon came up from hell and snatched him and took him straight to hell. The demon said, *"You keep calling my name, here I am. Every time you said my name you built a*

rung on this ladder from hell, straight to you."
Here's Johnny.

Do not simply repeat words that people tell you to say, you may not realize what hell you are summoning from the pit into your life, or into your death. Do not pay for a relationship with your life. Do not be that person.

Seriously, if you've just about lost your mind over a guy and especially if you don't know *why*, if you just feel some kind of way whenever you're around him, you need to be prayerful that you've haven't lost your mind and that *magic* of some sort is not involved. This kind of thing is rampant, folks.

The devil can empower a man to be charming and irresistible to women, especially if he has asked the devil for that, and has entered into evil covenant with the devil. He may have asked the devil for anything that he thinks would enchant women. Physical attributes, physical prowess, money, smarts, good looks, wit--, or just animal magnetism as they call it, a *seducing spirit*. Bedroom eyes, seducing, bewitching bedroom eyes. He may not have all those things, maybe just one of those things, but what he does have, he's working it on you. If you catch yourself saying you can't resist something about him, then it may have a ***demonic charge*** on it. It is not intended just for you, if he has it, he's using it on everyone he can.

He may have asked the devil for *charm*. That's a dangerous word; a charm is a spell cast on a person or an object to be used against another person's free will. Most of these men are so enchanted with their enchantments that they talk about it all the time. They brag on it. They walk with a swag that is over the top and if you ask them, they will talk about their body parts and abilities, even their shoe size if you let them. They are in love with sex, money, power, or all three. They have become an evil altar, either knowingly or unwittingly.

If you go to their altar to worship, **you** are the intended sacrifice, slowly or quickly. Don't be their sacrifice; don't be that person.

He may be irresistible to silly women, unsaved women, unsuspecting women, but not to you, right? If the devil had his way, he would deceive even God's very elect. Don't be that deceived woman.

If he's over the moon when he's with you, so much so that it's just unreal. It **is** unreal. He could be acting. Yup, just acting. Maybe you've never been groomed for anything. It is sensational. Delightful. Totally fulfilling. Until it's not. And it is not when he gets what he wants from you.

Spirit Spouse

Renegade *spirits* in your soul are *spirit spouses*. First thing they try to block is your relationship with God. They do not want you to prosper in Christ. (Gen 35). The next thing they fight, is your natural marriage-- 24/7 from your meeting the right person, dating them, engagement, the ceremony and the actual marriage. You **must** get rid of spirit spouses. Soonest!

Sex in the dream is a symptom of having a *spirit spouse*, but that does not always have to be the case. The purpose of it is, like the eating of spirit food is to defile you; God hates defilement. There are instances of having sex in the dream, but the entire dream is wiped, so nothing is remembered. You will need to pray fervently that the Holy Spirit helps you recall every detail of your dreams.

The most polygamous of all polygamous human mates is the one that has a *spirit spouse,* or MORE than one *spirit spouse,* whether they know it or not. Danger. Danger. If you have a *spirit spouse* that means a demon believes it is married to you. Either of you could have one or more *spirit spouses.*

From here to the end of this chapter is excerpted from my book, **Fantasy Spirit Spouse**, which mainly focuses on one of the more than 30 different types of *spirit spouse.* It's from the chapter entitled, *A Demon by Any Other Name.* A demon by any other name is still a demon.

Here's the list with brief descriptions that was promised:

Marine spirit spouse-- the majority of *spirit spouses* are from the evil water (marine kingdom). They look beautiful. Think of mermaids, mermen, or merfolk when thinking of these entities.

*Resident spirit spouse*s are disembodied beings, that believe that humans are their 'homes" or house. They usually squat there while people are sleeping or dreaming.

However, in the presence of God it is too hot for them. So, stay prayed up.

Giant spirit spouses are spiritual devil prostitutes, remnants from Genesis 6:6.

Serpentine spirit– snake *spirit spouses*. May appear as ½ human and ½ fish or ½ snake. Can look beautiful as queens or kings with crowns on their heads.

Ancestral spirit spouses pose as living or dead ancestors. They can be *familiar* and *monitoring spirits* and will sleep with any- or everyone in a family.

Physical spirit spouse- when a *spirit spouse* manifests as a physical human being. If you see someone who is too good looking to be true, beware. They can appear and disappear at will—even right before your eyes. You're not crazy – that really happened.

Projected spirit spouse- witch doctors, voodoo priests, occultists, use astral projection to have spiritual sex with a victim. (Eccl 12:6)

Fantasy or *Imagination spirit wife/husband*. Your mind, your imagination is the drawing board of your destiny, according to Minister Geoff Uzo. Usually, there is no memory of the sexual event in the victim; it has been wiped away, but there is physical evidence that sex actually happened.

Bloodline spirit spouses (lust, polygamy *spirit spouses*)– (genetic *spirit spouses*). Transferred from consensual sex before conception. **PRAY before you have relations with your own spouse.**

Idol spirit – a person attracts generational curses when they worship idol *gods* and end up being married to these idol *gods*. For example, all shamans have *spirit spouses*. They want them and believe that it helps them in their powers.

Dwarf spirit husband/wife- some women think these demons are their future children because of their size, but this is not so.

Disembodied spirit spouses are demons with no spiritual bodies. They define themselves in deliverance as, *"Nobody."*

Strongman spiritual spouse of generational and family curses. They sponsor other demons and control them. They call themselves the boss, the mighty, terrible, landlord, the leader. They store up people's blessings over the years in a spiritual strong room.

Leviathan spirit spouses are the old-world serpent in charge of water snakes, mermaids, mermen, and merfolk. Harder to dislodge. Need a seer who is prophetic and apostolic to get deliverance. Works with Asmodee (Asmodeus), a wicked sexual demon whose goal is to defile humans.

Animal spirit spouses. Animals are not meant to be seen in the dream. You have got to stay prayed up. Pray a wall of fire, a hedge of fire, a mountain of fire around you before sleep.

Strange man or strange woman spirit spouses physically attack natural spouses. The have and use powers such as telekinesis. These are the kind that horror movies are made of. They fly around and can move things around in the house—right before your very eyes.

Old man or old woman spirit spouses usually torment people of younger age with sex in the dream. Things rattle around, causing noises in the house and even pictures can fall off the wall. They make a young person look old, and then no one wants to marry them because their beauty is gone.

Transferred spirit spouses can come from working in deliverance and ministry, et cetera. Any possession, object or person can *transfer* spirits. To guard against this, DO NOT SHARE personal items with people--, nobody, not a best friend, not even a family member. Period.

Territorial spirit spouses. Every river, house, enclave or subdivision has ruling or territorial demons over those areas. They have legal right or authority to be there. Just because you can't see them, doesn't mean that they are not there and operating. They think they own everything including people in "their" area/territory.

Hermaphrodite spirit spouses show up as transgendered by whatever means that will work for the evil they plan to inflict on the victim. They can turn a woman into a man or turn a man into a woman and they become the gender required to attack them. They are vicious and violent.

Hidden spirit spouses don't even show up in the dream. They are not interested in sex in the dream. But they cause disease, tragedies, and block successes and breakthroughs.

Masquerading spirit spouses is the typical identity theft. They are crafty and tricky. They use the face of familiar people so that they will be accepted while you let down your guard and may consent to dream sex. Works with the *spirit of lust*. If you are the lusting type and someone, anyone presents to you with dream sex, you'll probably agree to it.

Multiple spirit spouses – when a person experiences more than one sexual partner during the dream. Gang stalkers. Gang rape. Group sex, orgy type sex in the dream.

Incestuous spirit spouses happen in magic, New Age, witchcraft type of homes. Some parents marry their own children to their "spirit guides" for power or for protection or rites of passage. It is all demonic.

Witchcraft or warlock spirit spouses when you consult a witchdoctor you get initiated whether you know it or not. You become a **blind witch** that means you are a witch and do not even know it. Period. A spirit spouse is assigned as soon as you visit anyone practicing in the dark arts.

Celebrity spirit spouses speaks for itself. Memorabilia has familiar spirits attached to them. It's all a masquerade though.

Transference spirit spouses—pastors, doctors, intercessors, et cetera should be mightily prayed up so this doesn't happen. Countertransference is possible also when the deliverance worker, pastor, doctor, massage therapist, et cetera transfers *their* demons to their clients/customers/patients. Best to stay prayed up and consider who you are putting your hands on and who is putting their hands on you. Sometimes touch is not even involved, some transference can happen just by being in association with a person and in their vicinity.

Manifested spirit spouses show up first in the dream, but later they take a human form and show up in the natural.

Graveyard spirit spouse or necromancer spirit spouses attach to a person from visiting cemeteries, graveyards, going to funerals, et cetera. Demons can follow folks home. Sometimes called stubborn pursuers. I've never once heard a person officiating a funeral pray for anything more than peace, comfort and strength to the family of the deceased. I've heard NO ONE ever pray for the general protection of the attendees at the memorial, wake, funeral or interment.

(In my book, **Ancestral Powers,** I have included such a prayer. https://a.co/d/4sH0VXW)

Desert spirit spouses can attach to people who are not prayed up but go to certain areas where demons have been displaced to.

Forest spirit spouses-, it depends on what kind of forest it is – if it's a dedicated forest or a dedicated grove, hikers, hunters, et cetera beware. These demons can follow people home, stalk them and become dream sex partners.

(This list comprised from Minister Geoff Uzo)

Grossed out yet? You should be.

Sex demons entrap, enslave, capture and ruin lives, destiny and the destinies of entire bloodlines.

Divorcing Spirit Spouse

Also in the book, **ESM, Evil Spirit Marriage** by Dr. Anthony Akerele https://a.co/d/1eNaJBO he speaks about the *gods* of our father's house, the *gods* of our ancestors that are requiring worship of us that we are not giving them because we are now saved. Yes, we said the sinner's prayer, but we can't just layer Jesus into our lives like so much waxy buildup on a floor. Did we strip that floor back to the natural wood, back to our essence *before* or when accepting Christ?

The sinner's prayer will get us saved, but what do we do about what we worshipped before receiving Christ? What do we do in the natural about all the people we've dated before we married the "love of our life?" Scattered memories remain even though we've said marriage vows in front of a pastor, a judge, or whomever. Which vow do we really mean? The first, the second, the next, or the last one? Is there a history of unfulfilled vows?

Maybe we didn't say an actual vow with the others, but our behavior initiated a contract that the idol *gods* are demanding service on. Maybe we didn't say or do anything, but our ancestors made a vow or an oath that constituted covenant with an idol *god* that still demands worship. Previous vows come back to haunt. It is better to not make a vow than to not fulfill one. (Eccl 5:5)

Every demon raising accusations against me in the spirit, receive the Blood of Jesus.

Every agreement and covenant, vow, pledge, oath that I have entered into in the past that is affecting my life today, be broken by the power of the Holy Ghost, in the Name of Jesus. I nullify every evil covenant that I have entered into in my juvenile or adult ignorance, in the Name of Jesus.

Spirit spouse has to go; it is very possessive and is known to block relationships and marriages. In dire cases I've heard of a *spirit spouse* as the very jealous physical spouse, who plans to not let go at any cost, even the cost of life. Do not put yourself in a position to have to pay for a relationship with life.

We read even today that there are those who become homicidal when they feel that their relationship is threatened. What comes over people? The ungodly are a blank canvas that the devil paints with ire, rage, even murder, at will. If a person has no defenses and no guards, evil *spirits* can jump in and out of a person, at will.

Recall in the Old Testament how an evil *spirit* would come over Saul? Once the *spirit* overcame Saul, he sought to kill David. This evil *spirit* in Saul chased David for decades because he was jealous of him. Jealousy is a cruel beast; when someone is jealous of someone they can behave irrationally, dangerously.

Guard yourself by only marrying someone who is saved, and submitted to the Holy Spirit so the walls of their city are guarded and demons cannot just come and go at will.

Spirit Children

If there is a *spirit spouse*, there are *spirit children*. As long as spirit children remain, spirit spouse won't leave. So, get rid of spirit children, first. Spirit children block the woman from having natural children. They hate and will torment your natural children, but their goal is to block you from having any natural children.

Spirit children are seen in the dream--, no that's not your future human child in the dream; that is a spirit child. In your dreams you may be handed a baby, see yourself pregnant, nursing a baby. That is an evil spirit child. Cancel that dream, in the Name of Jesus! Now do warfare against spirit children.

After that, get rid of spirit spouse. You have to be saved, a Protestant Christian who is fully committed to Christ and not someone just trying to layer Jesus into their life with a bunch of *idols*. A doubleminded man can expect to receive nothing from God.

So Much *Marine* Out There

Sometimes I have felt that all is left out there for relationships is *marine*. That could be that is all that is left. It could be that those who are left have been initiated or have realized that they are marine. Could be they are not marine, but are just behaving badly. Or the marine kingdom has inserted some fellows in for all the ladies who are looking, or desperately searching, hoping. As asked earlier, *Is he even human?*

This is not exhaustive, but here are some signs that he might be *marine*. He drinks, he could be an alcoholic or drug addict. He gambles, usually daily or at least weekly; he gambles a lot, on many different things, lottery, sports, almost anything. Gambling is why many men are addicted to sports – they've got

money on the game. They've got **money** on the fight.

He may have had at least one divorce, maybe multiple. Lots of girlfriends and exes, whether he tells you about them or not. If he's full of lust, he might be *marine*. Most lust demons come from the *water kingdom*. He probably is very good looking, it's a trait of the marine kingdom. If you think he's hot, and hot-blooded, a little freaky, loves pornography – that's *marine*.

To enter or remain in a relationship, the ultimatum needs to be, he either seeks salvation and deliverance, or you should run. If he gets saved today, it takes 3 years for fruit to develop and ripen. The Word says, *we shall know them by their fruit.*

I'm not judging anyone who is trapped in the *marine kingdom* generationally, or by their own doing, ignorantly, or not. Most who are in it were born into it; their ancestors had all the "fun" and the children inherited all the sin debt, the iniquity. Though they are ancestral demons, he needs deliverance. Before marriage would certainly be the wisest timing rather than you walking down the aisle to marry a man who is steeped in the *marine kingdom* which is full of fallen angels who force themselves on and defile the daughters of men (Gen 6:6), which God detests.

I think I've attracted more than my share of *marine*. Could it be because of **my** own ancestral foundation, which I've had to surmise to have *marine* influence?

Warning: Males who may not even be the father in a family who may have done a money ritual either in earnest, or because they thought it was a joke and nothing would happen anyway – and all their sisters are not married. This is another clue. This male seems to always have money, and his sisters always seem to *need* money. Yet another clue.

It's super commonplace, however; no one should want it in their bloodline or foundation. The marine kingdom influences music, fashion, makeup, hair. Isn't that pretty much **everyone? Isn't that** everyone who cares what they look like to any degree, but especially to the *nth* degree? I love music– doesn't everyone say that? So, pretty much everyone is influenced by the marine kingdom.

You must pray and fast big time. The Holy Spirit only knows if you've been a victim of a money ritual. The victim doesn't really have money but depends on the person who does have it and that person may be the reason you don't have money, but they do. Another case of the person who **caused** your hardship helping you through your hardship. How magnanimous.

Worse, whatever demon they are working with may suddenly demand a sacrifice. The person doing the money ritual won't volunteer *himself*.

Secrets

This is why you need to get to know your intended. It's not just to meet the relatives, although you should meet as many of them as possible. You must LEARN your intended. What are they about, what do they *do*? How do they think? Who or *what* do they worship? Are they available for a relationship, actually. Are they planning to be straightforward with you, or keep their secrets?

Look for secret rooms, mandatory man cave requests, and things you can't know about or see. Yes, everyone can have boundaries, but you will know in your spirit if he is being sneaky, just as he would know that in his spirit about you.

Previous Children

Is this yours or his second, or third, (or more) marriage? Has any spiritual work, divorce and the breaking of soul ties been done?

Children, as they should, will protect their inheritance, or their plans to receive inheritance, and may reject you.

If his ex or baby momma is really *that* bad, then get ready to meet Bae-Bae's kids. Here we go, they will be your step kids. Polygamous kids can be arch enemies; do you seriously want to put **your** kids through this? What if the kids are pitted against each other to hate each other? That's not always the case, but bitter wives, ex-wives, ex-girlfriends, witchy exes can be the source of a multitude of drama and **lifetime** problems for everyone involved.

Inheritance

As mentioned before, children will stop at nearly nothing to *protect* their dad from a new wife. Or, they are protecting their mother's feelings, if she's been abandoned. Moreover, they will stop at nothing to protect their inheritance that they are expecting from dad from who they may label as a gold-digging hussy. They'd be content for their dad to have no one, rather lose their inheritance, especially if she is younger and he might pre-decease her. Without a will, as the wife, she will get ½ and the children will split the other half in most states. If there's a will, she may get everything. The children, weighing that, may be thinking they will automatically get everything if he has no wife. If they are money grubbers, they will accuse a new wife of being exactly what they are--, human vultures and the man is not even on his sickbed.

When it comes to money and possible inheritance, often times siblings are just as bad or worse. By second or third marriage, parents may be part of the picture, some may not be. If there is one parent who has lived with that marriage candidate for many years, chances are they are not going to be so keen on you "taking" their child away from them.

Some years ago, I was accused of this by a 60-year-old woman who had another child and a doting husband, but she didn't want either of her two grown, 30-something children to leave home. Each did for a time, but then returned home to live to watch her to age 90, then she died. To this day they both live in the family home, alone--, neither of them with a spouse nor child.

Parents or siblings who are used to their relatives taking care of them may now see you as a threat, no matter how nice you are to them, will put up roadblocks to you having a relationship with their relative.

Perhaps you are a threat. Perhaps you are not. But they will still see you as a threat.

Marriage *Material*

How do you even get to *be* marriage material? I used to think that you've got that household thing down and you can take care of a man, a house, and a family. While you are busy working on becoming marriage material, what is he doing? Is *he* even marriage material? Is he even working on it?

He's living free and easy, dating proliferously, forming "marriages" when he believes he's doing the exact opposite—**avoiding marriage**. Yeah, he's avoiding it in the natural, but in the spirit, he's a serial polygamist.

I shudder to think how many "wives" the average man has who is out sowing his wild oats, since the usual goal is as many as possible. Also, I wonder how his *oats* got to be so wild in the first place. Second marriage, third? By the time you meet him, he's slept with 5 to 25, or more women. He's married to all of them unless he has divorced them spiritually and God allowed it. Yes, God allows divorce, but *til death* a marriage will last, til the death of a soul tie, a soul tie remains.

None of this is natural. How do I know that? Jesus was the perfect man. Even though we are shaped in iniquity and born into sin, that's not what God created. Adam was not whoremongering – Adam was not sinning until he sinned. The desire to chase anything, women, money, power, fame is of this world and not of God. Even though Adam threw off on Eve when God asked him about that sin, Adam did not complain to God that God had only given him **one** woman.

Is this boyfriend, fiancé, or intended a *freak*? What *else* will he ask you to do? If he doesn't get it from you, will he be in the streets? Unnatural desires are not of God; they are demonic. Where did he learn this stuff? In the streets? Porn?

Men love to accuse women of baggage, but they come into relationships with beaucoup spiritual baggage. The woman may carry a lot of "baggage" in her soul, in her emotions from the way she's been treated in previous relationships. Sometimes the woman's emotional baggage is in **response** to *his* spiritual baggage, but he's clueless that he's loaded to the gill with "**wives**." He's got 10 wives in his soul that he doesn't even realize he has, but they are making her feel very insecure.

It's more than when he's with you he may be thinking of someone else, entirely. He may be comparing this that or the other about you to *her*. He may be wishing for this experience or that experience, or trying to recreate a former experience. This is why it is best not to have all these *experiences*; you will forever be comparing and that is emotional adultery.

Oh, she'll never know you may think. Really? God will know and He has no place for adulterers because if you are going to be marrying His Son, don't you think He'll be seriously vetting you? Adultery is a work of the flesh and those who participate in it will not inherit the Kingdom.

With Permission

I recall living in a town where everywhere I went some guy was checking me out. I later moved to another town where **no one** saw me. Was it the town, or was it me? Was it the timing of my life? Was it what had become *attached* to me? Did I have a *spirit spouse* back then and not even know it? Was there a covering cast or an evil veil over me so no one saw me? As a person looking to be married, do you realize now how much spiritual work must be done to even become marriage material--, to even be seen?

By location, we must ask: was that area even open for me to find a spouse and get married? Right now, we must look into the ability to become *marriage material* based on your **location**.

I'm ever amazed that young people think the world is their oyster, they will go pretty much anywhere at any time. If a plane, train, automobile or ship is going there, they don't mind getting on it. They choose countries to live in for a few years just for fun or for the experience of it.

I'm not sure how I feel about that, but it's not my decision where they go or choose to live. But the question becomes is that *land* where they are moving to live even welcoming and friendly to them? This may be evidenced by the reception they get – not the tourists' welcome, but how you are really received if you are going to domicile in a country.

Many countries have strict rules of citizenship for expats. Some countries, especially the islands, which I'm sure are very popular, won't let you buy a house there, some won't let you work there, some only will let you work there; you cannot go there to retire, for example. Some will let you live there if you are buying a house that cost at least $400K, for example. That's all in the natural.

But how do you know if a land is *spiritually* open to you for you to live there, work there, prosper and even marry or enjoy marriage there? Every tourist's welcome is lovely, it's money in their pockets. One man I know wants to revisit a certain country because he states that the women treat you like a king there. Why he needs to be treated like a king, I'm not really sure. But he's only seen the tourist side of that country and does not realize it. I pray for him.

> It was reported to the king of Assyria: "The people you deported and resettled in the towns of Samaria do not know what the god of that country requires. He has sent lions among them, which are killing them off, because the people do not know what he requires."
> Then the king of Assyria gave this order: "Have one of the priests you took captive from Samaria go back to live there and teach the people what the god of the land requires." So one of the priests who had been exiled from Samaria came to live in Bethel and taught them how to worship the LORD. (1 Kings 17:26-28)

Growing up, my brothers told me, and I believe them, that there was a neighboring county that if you were a boy from another county, after dark, you were run out of that town. Period. The neighboring boys did not have permission to even date, much less, *marry* the girls of that particular county.

If the land you live in, or the land he lives in is not allowing you, or that man to marry, you will have a battle on your hands. You must be in the right place and places in your life. You must be where God has commanded the blessings for you. If you are in a strange land, or a land that is not accepting of you, things will not work out socially, in business or career, or in family or marriage. How did you happen to come to that land? Were you born there? What does God say about you being there, or where you should be. There are territorial demons that fight your progress if you are not allowed in a land. Even Jesus came up against that. Can any good thing come out of Nazareth? (because of territorial powers) locking, blocking people out of blessings. You pray. Find out where destiny means you to be. Where your Kingdom spouse is. Find out where you are supposed to be living right now or for your whole life. That is where God will strengthen, settle, and establish you. Your Rehoboth is the place where the Lord will make room for you. **Amen.**

Pro-Marriage

Please don't think I'm anti-marriage. I am not. I am pro-marriage. I believe in God, I believe in covenant, and I believe that the Church will be married to the Lamb, ultimately. For this reason, marriage on Earth is the best practice we can have for that Godly union that we all seek.

I used to think that staying married was a matter of willpower and sheer determination. Oh, I know so much more now. It takes so much more than that.

So why is the divorce rate more than 50%? Hosea 4:6 says, My people are destroyed for a lack of knowledge. Marriages are also destroyed for a lack of knowledge. Marriage is a spiritual union, so you need spiritual knowledge to endure. You could have determination and sheer luck. There could be other "powers" working to keep a marriage together or a marriage may look like it's together and may not be together at all.

This book is so your eyes can be open, wide open. With legal divorce rates so high, and people, especially women losing their lives because of marrying an enemy instead of a friend or a lover, I had to pen this book.

Prayers

Who must agree that I can be married, and you are not Jehovah, die, in the Name of Jesus.

Who must agree that I can get married, stay married and have a happy marriage, and you are not Christ, die, in the Name of Jesus.

In-law witchcraft, die, in the Name of Jesus.

Polygamous witchcraft, die, in Jesus' Name.

Permission to get married, stay married and be happy in marriage in the hands of the wicked, be withdrawn, in the Name of Jesus.

Permission to get married, stay married and be happy in marriage in the hands of the gods of my father's house, die, in the Name of Jesus.

Every word curse over my relationship, engagement, or marriage, break, by the power in the Blood of Jesus. Amen.

If my name is such that I cannot get married, stay married, and be happy in marriage, I have a new name in Christ and I stake a claim, in the Name of Jesus.

If my blood is such that I cannot own land or property, Blood of Jesus remove my blood and replace it with the Blood of Jesus, Amen.

Powers assigned to release bad people into my life, die in the Name of Jesus.

Oh God arise and release the right people into my life, in the Name of Jesus.

The idols by whose actions and plans I get rejected and disappointed in relationships, die and let your altars die, in the Name of Jesus.

Prayers Against Late Marriage/ Marital Delay

Help me Lord to know myself. Search me, my heart…

Let every imagination of the enemy against my marital life be rendered impotent, in the Name of Jesus.

I reject every anti-marriage spell against me, in the Name of Jesus.

I cancel every bewitchment against my getting married, staying married and being happy in marriage, in the Name of Jesus.

Lord, let every force bringing the wrong people into my life be paralyzed, in the Name of Jesus.

I command all forces of evil delaying or hindering my marriage to be completely paralyzed and stopped, in the Name of Jesus.

I break every covenant of marital failure and late marriage, in the Name of Jesus.

Let all evil anti-marriage marks be removed in Jesus' Name.

I cancel every spiritual wedding involving me, conducted consciously or unconsciously in the Name of Jesus.

Lord, restore me to the perfect way in which You created me, if I've been altered, in the Name of Jesus.

Household wickedness against my marriage: stand down. (X3), or receive the wrath of God.

Let every incantation, incision, hex, or vex working against me be completely neutralized, in the Name of Jesus.

Lord, expose all the schemes of the enemy against me and my marriage, in the Name of Jesus.

Lord forgive me for all personal sin that has given ground to the enemy, especially sexual sin, in the Name of Jesus.

I break all satanic connections and any linkage to strange people, in the Name of Jesus.

I remove the right of the enemy to block me from getting married by the power in the Blood of Jesus.

Angels of the Only Living God, remove every blockage to my marital breakthrough, in the Name of Jesus.

All masquerading *spirits* troubling my marital life be bound in the Name of Jesus.

I receive my Kingdom match, in the Name of Jesus. Fire of God, melt away any obstacle to my marriage and marital blessings, in the Name of Jesus.

Lord, give me my Rehoboth, the land where God has made room for me, for marriage, for victory, success, and destiny, in Jesus' Name.

Lord, turn away all that will jilt, disappoint or fail me, in the Name of Jesus.

Lord, send me a spouse that will not neglect the family prayer altar, in the Name of Jesus. Lord with your divine axe cut down all my problems at the root, in the Name of Jesus.

Finger of God, pull down every stronghold up against me, in the Name of Jesus.

Lord, let my home be released from every evil, in the Name of Jesus.

Holy Spirit redirect every evil wind sent against my home and marriage in the Name of Jesus.

Prosperity in finances, health and marriage, come into my life, home and relationship today, in the Name of Jesus.

Lord, I stand in the gap and I go ahead of every potential problem that could result from a second, third or any marriage in the Name of Jesus. I bind up every retaliatory spirit and command all backlash against me because of these prayers to backfire in the Name of Jesus.

I seal these declarations across every age, realm, dimension, and timeline, past, present, and future, in the Mighty Name of Jesus Christ.

AMEN.

Christian books by this author

AK: Adventures of the Agape Kid

AMONG SOME THIEVES

Ancestral Powers

As My Soul Prospers

Behave

Churchzilla (Wanna-Be Bride of Christ)

The Coco-So-So Correct Show

Demonic Cobwebs

Demonic Time Bombs

Demons Hate Questions

Do Not Orphan Your Seed

Do Not Work for Money

Don't Refuse Me Lord

Every Evil Bird

Evil Touch

The FAT Demons

got Money?

Let Me Have a Dollar's Worth

Living for the NOW of God

Lord, Help My Debt

Lose My Location

Made Perfect In Love

The Man Safari *(I'm Just Looking)*

Marriage Ed., *Rules of Engagement & Marriage*

Motherboard: *Key to Soul Prosperity*

My Life As A Slave

Name Your Seed

Plantation Souls

The Poor Attitudes of Money

Power Money: Nine Times the Tithe

The Power of Wealth

Seasons of Grief

Seasons of War

Second Marriage, Third Marriage any Marriage

SOULS in Captivity

Soul Prosperity: Your Health & Your Wealth

The *spirit* of Poverty

This Is *NOT* That

The Throne of Grace, *Courtroom Prayers*

Warfare Prayer Against Poverty

When the Devourer is Rebuked

The Wilderness Romance

Other Journals & Devotionals by this author:
The Cool of the Day – Journal
got HEALING? Verses for Life
got HOPE? Verses for Life
got WISDOM? Verses for Life
got GRACE? Verses for Life
got JOY? Verses for Life
got LOVE? Verses for Life
He Hears Us, Prayer Journal
I Have A Star, Dream Journal
I Have A Star, Guided Prayer Journal,
J'ai une Etoile, Journal des Reves
Let Her Dream, Dream Journal *in colors*
Men Shall Dream, Dream Journal,
My Favorite Prayers (in 4 styles)
My Sowing Journal
Tengo una Estrella, Diario de Sueños
Illustrated children's books by Dr. Miles
Big Dog (8-book series)

Do Not Say That to Me

Every Apple

Fluff the Clouds

I Love You All Over the World

Imma Dance

The Jump Rope

Kiss the Sun

The Masked Man

Not During a Pandemic

Push the Wind

Tangled Taffy

What If?

Wiggle, Wiggle; Giggle, Giggle

Worry About Yourself

You Did Not Say Goodbye to Me

www.ingramcontent.com/pod-product-compliance
Lightning Source LLC
Chambersburg PA
CBHW061336040426
42444CB00011B/2946